My In

Book 1:
Red Sky at Night

Charles Browne

About the author

Charles Browne was born in Lambeth Hospital in 1966. He grew up in a large house with a big family and as a boy was sociable and athletic. Aged 9 Charles' family divided and he, his mother and brother moved to a small flat. A thoughtful dreamer, exams weren't his forte, so he left school at 17, not sure what to do.

Around this time, hanging out with friends and plugged into his Walkman, Charles first started to experience paranoia. He dabbled in different jobs and aged 19 he began training to be an Optical Technician.

When Charles first started hearing voices he didn't tell a soul. When he finally shared his concerns and was prescribed medication, he overdosed and found himself in a psychiatric hospital. Life was never the same again. Charles worked in various opticians until 1994 with short periods of work following, but life became a haze of drop-in centres and hospitals.

In 2005 Charles had a serious breakdown and ended up in various hospitals for two years. It was at this time that he started writing poetry. Dark and troubled months ensued but he came out the other side. Charles has been a volunteer at Blackfriars Settlement for over 10 years. He has been a part of a poetry group at CoolTan Arts for the last 7 years. Charles is a father. Charles is a poet.

"Here I am now 2015 still paranoid, still hearing voices, still trying to be a good dad, still at CoolTan Arts, still at Blackfriars Settlement volunteering. I have amazed myself with my resilience over the years from illness to illness, panic attacks to panic attacks from my anger at the world and myself to still being on this earth to have a chance to really live again."

Introduction

We have known Charles Browne at Blackfriars Settlement for over ten years. Blackfriars Settlement, a registered charity, is a community care organisation that enhances the lives of local people of all ages. Charles Browne first joined us as a member of our Mental Health and Wellbeing Services. He attended the Wednesday sessions and made many friends. Then he was introduced to older people's services by a friend and signed up as a volunteer for our Crusoe Club for the blind on Fridays.

His charming personality won the hearts of club members and staff alike. He has tirelessly and unconditionally given his time over many years to enlighten the lives of our most vulnerable group of older people. Even after club hours Charles visits an isolated member to make sure she feels included. He is always at hand if anyone needs help - it was no trouble for Charles to take a visually impaired member to see her favourite opera at the Royal Albert Hall. Charles also runs our "Forget Me Not" club session on Tuesdays. This session is for older people with memory problems, to engage in memory games and crosswords.

We were aware of Charles Browne's talents in writing poetry for many years. On several occasions we have been so proud to have Charles recite his poems to our club members. I feel personally privileged to have Charles Browne in my volunteer team. I am aware of his mental health condition and have tried my best to support him at the times he has needed us the most. During a long spell that he was in hospital I made sure I visited him and always encouraged him to bring out his feelings in poetry.

Charles got into the habit of emailing his poems to me. I started saving them in a folder and in 2014, I realised that it was time to put Charles's poems into a book so that everyone can read, enjoy and feel the "Inspirational Mind" of Charles Browne in the same way that we do. Charles has written hundreds of poems, so we decided to print his books in a series. This first volume, "Red Sky at Night", includes 150 of his poems.

You will see a variety of themes. Some may take you to a darker place while others will get your mind thinking and even put a smile on your face. Charles Browne is a champion for people with mental health problems and an example to us all. This talented man takes us deep into his mind and lets us share his thoughts. I feel it is time we introduced him to all poetry lovers. It is indeed my privilege to have the fortune of supporting the printing of his first book.

Tina Johnston,
Coordinator for Older People's Services
Blackfriars Settlement

Dedication

I dedicate "Red Sky at Night", my first book, to my mother, Doreen Elaine Browne who supported me all through my troubled years.

Acknowledgements

Thank you to:

Tina Johnston for supporting me and giving me encouragement for my inspirational mind.
Blackfriars Settlement - for being the umbrella for all to come together to make a dream a reality
Bernadette Macanlalay - for taking time to enter all the poems in the first draft .
Truly Johnston - for the front cover photo and editing.
Lucy Ismail - for proof reading.
David Johnston - for his support and encouragement and part funding the book.
John Pannell - for organising the final draft for printing of the book, setting up and promoting Red Sky at Night.

Red Sky at Night

I hear the distance of war
Trumpets that pound out the light,
Never so close but o so far
I hear the trumpets shepherd the night.

Flashes of cries passing by
Clouded the mists of night
Rain falling down as moist screams
Blooded the sky, red by night.

Trumpets fell silent I hear,
Trouble blew over a storm,
Bodies strewn over the fields,
Clutching each other, by dawn.

Someone's someone

Depressive this journey
Wheels cog up around
As the sky falls slowly over,
Many a man had gone
Over the top to nowhere land
Same old routine
Made the fantasy of getting home
Harder to visualize.
I've seen with eyes peeled
Men get shot in the foot
But by their very own hand
To stop the torture, stop the rot.
I've seen my mate Tommy
Gun down thousands
And always wondered
The letters home, the tears cried.
For they were all someone's sons,
Someone's someone,
As I am just a man
Trying to get home
As best I can.

I am the one

I am the one who
Fodders the land
for girls to lay
And cry in hand.

I am the one who,
with fearless heart
Bayonets the Kaiser
With pointed sharp.

I am the one who
Hears homeward screams
If not in box
With shattered dreams.

I am the one who
Had never learnt
From my life's birth,
till I killed my first.

A night on the tiles

"Never go there again,"
Was my chant in the morning?
Head bursting with the over.
Hanging out to dry
From a night on the tiles
And all its misdemeanours.
Couldn't hold down
Bacon, Eggs, and two Hash Browns,
Remember snippets
Like Polaroid pictures
Snapped was the evidence
Of last night's disobediences.

Picture is Silence

Time will tell as the bells toll
For forward men to speak
Of the unspeakable truth behind
The facade that was the Brigade
That lightly charged.

Many were sent to their slaughter
Even tho, they should have been
Back in the bosom of their
Sons and daughters,
"Back before you know it poppet,"
Didn't ring true as only a few
Would tell the tale, but let
History speak for itself, lightly.

Beware

I liked the sound the words
Scaly Eyed Wombat made,
I liked them so much
Looked it up in a exotic book.
And in it, it said,
If the sky is red at night
Near to an Old Oak Tree,
Beware the Scaly Eyed Wombat.

The Curious Audacity of Mr. Darcy

The curious audacity
Of Mr. Darcy
Was hard to comprehend.

With his ability
That Mr. Darcy
Was at it again.

Like Jekyll and Hyde
Was hard to like
After killing his wives.

Turned out number five
Outlived his life as he
Was hung out to dry.

Our Love

She moves me,
Even more than a mountain can.
Separate us,
And I'm lost in the wilderness.

She warms me,
With her winter's smile.
Melting pot
As our souls collide.

Calms me,
When scarlet is my phase.
Doomsday,
When I leave her side.

Understands me,
More than any other.
Infuriates me,
Moved to distraction.

Thunderous,
Let no one put asunder.
Our love,
Keeps us in-tuned, entwined, together.

Owl and the Pussycat

Said Owl to the Pussycat,
You're a beautiful dream
That I had once
Or twice so it seems.
We did sail off
In a pea green boat
But did capsize
Still kept afloat.

Pussy said to Owl
How charming you were
To sing as we bobbed
In the waves far from shore.
And by mercy were saved
Drifting off from your tune
And were married next eve
By the light of the moon.

Cream of the Cat

The cat that got the cream
Beamed with delight
Whiskers white looking wise
As its master saw it
otherwise.

Writers block

I . . . . .

Unchained Slavery

Slavery seems so far away,
But were afflicted and chained
From back in the centuries
Right up to the present day.
Lost on the underground now
But scratch the surface
And deep down below
The dirt escalates to molehills.

Blacked Out

The problem with living in the basement is
Everyone has to come down to your level.
Cornerstones are lit up while every
Chickin' Lickin' only gets to third base
Before conking out. You dream of coming up
To see the sunset but end up going back down
Underground for one last homeward shot.
"One day," you say, but cloud your vision with
The thought of the Windrush feeling,
That breeze, in your hair without a care
For an hour or two anyway
Keeping you in the mood.

The problem tho with living in the basement is
You have lucid dreams played out in the shadows
In corners of your mind, that until you let go of
Will always be that, because.....

Far from the Maddening Crowd

Let out for half an hour
From the maddening crowd,
So sat down in the park to eat.

Then I noticed the bench
Had an inscription so I read it,
"Please leave as you would like to find."

And I wasn't feeling that great so,
I left my sandwiches smeared all over it.

I Know It, So It Is

I know it, so it is,
Isn't it?
I know that for certain
Surely, I'm sure of that,
That's for certain
Because that is what I know.
And if I didn't
I'd still be certain of that
Because I'd still know that
For certain, for sure that I didn't.

"ill" Manners

Hard to get off the carousel
Once you're on it, concrete slabs
For cold hearted warriors who
Battle for turf for it's their nature.
Something to do on a cold cold
Evening, flashing the blade
Cross the chest of
A former mate from the estate.
A statement of intent,
A statement to suggest don't mess with us
Or else we'll turn on you,
Imploding slowly within our
"ill" manners.

Who the Cap Fits

Life was hard in the fifties
When we come from abroad,
Treated same as de Irish,
Cat, Dawg oh my lord.
Came here for a better life
Struggled but we still strived
Misunderstood by all de whites
So gave ourselves high fives.

Took all de jobs
De whitey didn't want
Then hated and berated
Cos we mek a few bob.
But we stuck at it
The first few years I'm told
Were traumatic, but our autopilot
Kept us level headed and optimistic.

Second generation
Skanked da nation,
Till death us do part
Were their mixed blessings.
Rich pickings
Were their motivation
Carnival lickings
Kept dem vibrating.

See divide and rule
Wasn't shown to them at school
So we learnt on da streets
Dat ya rep was ya speech.

But what comes around
Goes way back around I guess,
Now here in little England
It's Eastern Europeans we cuss,
"Where will it stop," we say
But we haven't learnt a lot.
For we years ago were
Them very same people who flock,
So isn't that calling
The kettle the pot?

So just look back when judging
We're all lacking our fathers givings,
And if we understand this, maybe,
Just maybe, we'll understand
That a one-size cap fits all
No matter where we come from.

Automation

Like sheep we are but most don't realize
And the ones that stand up get chastised.

Don't rock the boat or we'll all drown,
Just go about your business
Blindly with automation.

Clock in, clock out,
That's what its all about.
Until our demise, only then
Do the sheep realise.

Dangerous Times

Dangerous Dan entered the saloon with a
clang,
Looked around and walked slowly as his
spurs sang.
Beady eyed he spied around for his nemesis
That Dapper Dan The Raw-Hide Man,
Who had stolen his Lady Love
Lucy Lash from his gun hand.

He clutched his gun ready for action,
no-one made a sound.
But Dapper Dan The Raw-Hide Man
Was nowhere to be found.
So off, he was gone,
Whiskey guzzled down in a flash,
Outward bound on the Deadwood Stage
Still hunting for Dapper
And his Lady Love Lucy Lash.

The Fallen

Don't really think I take in
The remembrance day hymns,
Or what it really stands for.
11th month, 11th day of the 11th hour
When all fall silent
In remembrance of the fallen.
When millions lost their lives
And millions formed disowned homes,
But as I get older and
Have more time to ponder,
I appreciate more often
The bravery of the fallen.

A Tidy Death

I enter his shrine,
Shoes laid out
All in a row
Wall to wall
Cupboard space
Every 7 minutes
Air freshener bursting thru.

Just like him
To keep it all tidy,
Just like him
To keep it all brief,
Just like him
To make no waves
By dying in his sleep.

I leave his shrine,
Head turned as I go
Remembering when
Laughter filled the room.
With just one remnant
I clutch the pieces left,
From his past cold, cold hand
From his untimely tidy death.

Crossed Lines

Across the beaten track
A cross was his burden,
A crossed word did him in
Said the Rabbi to the Roman.

2.4 Children

I'm the 0.4
Only five foot no half
Don't pigeon hole me tho
Get a smack in the mouth.
Double jointed
Patriotic yet tainted
Runt of the litter
Never ever was breast fed.
Just 0.4
Emphasizing the point,
Last of the siblings
First one to dislike.

Ascending

I lay on my bed
Thinking ahead
To tomorrow's frown,
I rise in the morning
And thru my day
Periodically get down.

I go to work
I come back home
Repetitive syndrome,
Weekends I play
The day away
But mostly on my own.

I'll keep a smile
For just in case
I'm feeling really down,
Now I'm ascending
No place for ending
My life before me now.

School Colours

Were you a red or a blue
Or of a tangerine hue,
School colours made you
A statement of rules.
Crop not too long with
Not too much grease on
And shoes shiny bright
Always as black as night.
With white cotton shirts on
That girls matched with skirts
All wares just to fit in
To conform, for assimilation.

Peter Pan

The childhood I never had
Is all wrapped up in my many years later,
Tantrums and biting the bit,
With frustrations of life I missed as a kid
Have me acting it out with family open
mouthed.
"He's having one of his turns again,"
Remembering way back when,
"Why won't you grow up?"
Family, friends and partners are all
Aggrieved and agreed upon,
"Then let's treat him like one."
But I state in the world of today
With all its aches and pains
Why would you want to grow up.

Be Still

Sunday morning and in bed at peace,
Away from all the hustle and bustle
Of a Monday to Friday.
Away from all the shopping
Of a Saturday morning,
A blue rinse here some keep fit there.

So still can hear Big Ben singing, stirring
From a distance, know all is well and calm
When this happens.
Think the world away, put it all right,
This fine Sunday morn
In bed and at peace.

Makes Sense

To avoid the long arm of the law,
Cut off your hands
So there's no use for
Handcuffs or other constraints
To lead you to your jailer.

Truck Driver's Lament

A chunky Yorkie for me
No puff pastry,
A man's man this trucker
All 10-4 and good buddy.

A loner in the making
On metal trams,
Sleep when a taken
On back seat divans.

All cats' eyes
White line chasing with
Matchsticks propping up
Until destination's saviour.

Whatever the Weather

Whether it be fair or foul
Whether it sleet fast or slow,
Teem down or spittle to the floor
The weather knows no relenting.
Cause strawberry jams
Or slow lane passing
The weather keeps us asking,
It never pauses
Always causing mischief.

Whether it be hot, hot, hot
Or leaves on the track
Watery or slippery
Everything swelters to a stop.
With frosty welcomes
Cold to the touch
Weather's always changing, rearranging,
Whether we like it or not.

There's a Moose Loose

"There's a Moose loose,"
Said the Elk that belched.
"Where in the house?"
Said the Pig who took a spirits swig.
"Under the stairs,"
Said the Magpies in pairs,
"Under the stairs."
But Hippo said, "No!"
Bout the Moose loose in the house,
"So if he's not there its a spirit in-nit?"
Said Jackass.
"Only for Elk's eyes tho
Mirrored back at him,"
Said the wise old Owl.

Grave Matter

Like the first Buds of May
My first hairs were my proudest,
As in, wanting to be a mature cheddar
Rather than a mild child, penciling in
Sometimes looked authentic
But I knew I wasn't the real deal.

Then they blossomed into sprouting mushrooms
With a never ending threshing of the crop
Really became monotonous to my sensitive touch.

But when the weeds came they were
The most humbling, knowing I was becoming
distinguished
Never again to see the first Buds of May,
Just grey matter.

Lift the Spirits

I can see it now my gran and grandad
Skipping the light Fandango, well
Trying to but to me they seem rooted
To the spot moving back and forth
And around.
It's always the same way
With the same tune playing
And the same old gentle faces,
No need to remember hard, seems like
Yesterday.
Tear jerk to the apple of my eye I'd find
When I back rewind to the good old days.
That was when you knew what was what,
And always had that safety net
When they were around and around
And around.

Most Unusual

The most unusual thing
That I ever stole was,
The air that I breathe.

Algebra

The mathematical context
Of the alphabet
Is my piece of the Pi.

Gone to the Dogs

Carrots are blind
But life goes on,
Faces are blushed
With wind swept hushes.

Puppies just sit and wait
While cats,
Well cats are
The dogs bollocks.

Alter Negro

My other self doesn't take any shit
And knows all the right ways of wit.
Roars of laughter he knows
Are not against him, but with him,
With warm smiles so kind to his skin.

Keeping Up with the Joneses

My neighbour's son got a gun for Christmas
So mine got a ray gun from Mars,
My neighbour's wife got a motorbike
So my other son Mike got a brand new car.

My neighbour's vice was to stay up all night
At the Dog and Thistle.
So I bought that pub to keep up with Rob and now,
I'm flat broke.

Misty Haze

When I was a child I was very vague,
A misty haze I've also turned into.
In a conversation I'd feel invisible
No one watching me, especially
As I'm like a crane and as a crane
You reign above the clouds.
The rain never affects the crane
But the above always feels left out in the rain.

Juicy

Pomegranates ruby but only on Tuesdays
Oranges are juicy to colour me in,
I'm feeling Bananas like a wet slippery fish
O.K. tho Peachy no crack to my dish.

Hard Lines

Shell shocked rocked
Can't hear anything,
Just see runners everywhere
From the corner of my eye.

That face, that face in front
My enemy, my great enemy,
Looks harmless enough
But his lines tell the tale,
Why am I here? they say,
Why has it come to this?
Couldn't be too long dead
And I'm soon to follow
In my enemies' footsteps.

Looks like an uncle of mine
A cheeky chappy, one who
Would be the soul of the party.
Wish we could have met
Under different circumstances,
But yet we have, and soon
to meet again away from this melee.

Thing of None-sense

To be nothing must have come from
Someone or something.
The big bang theory where they say
Our time began, really!
What was there before?
Therefore nothing I say
Must have some substance.

Trapped

Most people don't see what I see
When walking down the street,
I watch people mumbling
And think it's about me
Wrongly or rightly. The glances,
The stares, the I'm watching you there,
The let's make him uncomfortable
Until he can't bear it. See him on his toes
With roars of laughter, until
The next time of chapter's paranoia.

Zulu Dawn

"Take that back young man," I said,
"Or it'll be pistols this dawn."
"More like handbags by the look of ya,"
He replied.
"That's it I require satisfaction," I grunted,
Looking stared fixed at him and his second,
Their heads together mumbling for a moment
Then, talking with head bowed he said,
"SORRY, I didn't know it was you,
I'm deeply sorry no offence meant."
"Apology accepted young scamp," I replied,
"But be careful in future you never know
Who you are talking to."

Last Rites

It's going over and over in my mind,
How could I have been so unkindly?
A flippant word said in haste
Turned out to be my last blast.
Why did I have to raise my voice?
Why did it have so much venom?
Thinking if only, if only,
If only we could have parted friendly
Would not be left with the if only's.

Way Back When

When I was much younger thought I was the Pipe-
Piper,
With family crammed like a score in a van
In a house fit for a king but needing much
attention.

Me and bruv were Lord of the Flies of our manor
As in, every summer with our rolled up newspaper
Swatting whatever came in.

As for being the Pipe-Piper,
Every nightfall seemed to draw out my biggest
obstacles
Which were the smallest of fellows, some of
whom
Would be sprawled on the floor at dawn
Poisoned by mum's concoctions.

I'd lead survivors with moon as bait,
Trapped by their tails of woe I was truly musical.
I remember their performances my biggest
obstacles
As they danced to my merry tune.

Whats the Story Morning Glory

Gillian was full of joy
As she skipped down the road
Humming a throw away tune
In time to her skipping.
It was a nice sunny day
A Sunday a day to be gay,
Nearly reaching her destination
She sights her friend.
"Jackanory," He looks and smiles,
"Come with me Gillian,
I have to go up the hill
To the well for my mother."
On the way Jack told some tall tales,
Hence his nickname.

On the way back down
Jack tripped and tumbled, silly boy,
Too busy telling tall stories.
Gillian dusted him off
And home they foxed
As Jack felt a bit groggy.
"Mother will know what to do,"
And sure enough she did,
Bandaging him lovingly and tenderly.

Better-specs

From the morning after punch drunkenly
I have the mother of all headaches
Idling down the stairs for coffee's saviour
Hallelujah, for now I dehydrate
But concentrate on getting down safely.
Made it thru yesterday unscathed
But now I couldn't hack my usual tea,
But that's weird, everything seems strange
Then I remember it's last night's house.
Must put on my glasses and get the hell
away.

Faithful

Loneliness overwhelms me,
Heartache always finds me,
Pain runs and overtakes me
And sorrow, I know it well.

But faith never leaves me,
Hope grows around the corner,
And what pumps my veins is love
Love spilling over.

Casualties of war

Back when we use to play Doctors and
Nurses,
It was a game I think as kids wink
When the Stethoscope was placed on the
chest,
Revealing skin that was well covered
When adults did it for real. Funny tho,
That giggles would ensue when the Doc said,
Boy take down your trousers,
Or girls take off your blouses. It's all a game
to us kids
So why take it so seriously you adults, I
mean,
You should play like us kids,
When we talk about death's door we.....

Mother Nature, Father Time

If ya nah care mother nature
She gon catch ya, and bite ya,
Den father time will step in
And finish off what she start tah.

Ya nah tek care of this earth
Sodom and Gomorrah gon sweep thru
Bag you up, den
Chuck ya in dem rubbish shoot.

Delilah gon tempt ya,
Goliath gon threat ya,
So please give praises
And Jah will be wid ya
From ya very first step
Till ya very last breath.

Complainer

I used to complain about voices
Until they were gone, then,
I complained about money
Then trust, then life
The list goes on.
Really tho the only thing
That's needed is love,
Then all the other things
Just wither to dust.

What's the 411

"What's the 411?" said my son,
"The 411 is a drama to stay calmer,"
I replied. "Explain," he said
Inquisitively listening keenly,
"I want to enjoy the fun of the 411."
"It's simple I'll break it down,
It's when you were born,
The 4th of the 1st two-thousand and 1,
The day my life truly begun
With the fun of the 411.

Why is the Point

Why point that weapon
With more venom for me
Than the ones
That enslaved thee?

Don't know , well I do.

Scared to be unified
And denied the right
By all the whites who
Keep us fighting each other.

Why would you want to shop
Just in Asian shops
When your brother man
Is just hanging on?

Don't know, well I do.

Easier to see someone
From another community
Set free than give a
Hand up to a brother man.

If you don't know why
Certain things are,
Take a step back sometimes
Like I do.

England's West Ends

O woe is me the end is near
The sight to see its majesty,
Can see its strain I cannot bear
To see it plunge ungracefully.

The east I see looks on with glee
Opposing west end's stronghold,
Causing mayhem and calamity
With bombs so vile and bold.

What happened to diplomacy?
Or to love thy fellow man,
This world will end up in catastrophe
With nothing left but grains.

Now panic is east's havoc
Over west a proud all a conquering,
East dangles blasts of furious carrots
To depths of doom a spiralling.

Ultimate Affluence

I'm a negative eccentric collaborate
Of all that's insulate you see,
Trying to be a positive eclectic cohabitant
Of all that's relevant to me.
With all these things I'm easily palpable
Mind washed, mind turned from rubble,
But will be able, and will be capable
Of facing out my troubles.

My Ic's, My Aches, My Pains

Can't stand it pedantic
Can't stand me so frantic
About it a fanatic
Nothing doing tho just static.

My flow ebbs erratic
And seems o so tragic
Comical even an epic
Hysterical and in turmoil.

I'm angry and ballistic
Feeling old like a relic
But now just statistics
On other peoples lyrics.

Must say now don't mimic
So now back to basics
To repair from being drained
Of my Ic's, my aches, my pains.

Demonic Creatures

What form and void
With its grey colour that catches night,
The emptiness in its eyes
Is just as dark as its substance.
Hanging around upside down
With its senses heightened
As its victim's blood boils.

Time

The winds of time
Can quell your mind,
The winds of time
Can change you find.

The sands of time
Descend and fall,
The sands of time
Are grains absolved.

The length of time
Seems stretched apart,
The length of time
Keeps up the stars.

The end of time
Will we ever see,
The end of time
Neverendingly.

Seasons opposites

I would spring to your defence
My summer madness
Autumn I always fall
To winter's days of sadness.

My summer's warmth
My spring that never bends
I fall into your autumn
My always winter's friend.

Chores

Why is pressing so depressing?
All that ironing so depleting,
The washing up is always
An eternity of cleaning cups
Plates and bowls such
When down just seem so much.
These chores we have oil the wheels
As in, shapes our everyday routines.

Summer Heat

O fair maidens with
Flowers blooming by their side,
Walking legs eleven
Must then be summertime.
On show then akimbo
Out of hibernation,
Strutting then in stiletto heels
For summer's sake of fashion.
On life's stage then all for show
All dressy and a wondrous bright,
Like colours flashing of a rainbow
O please not come the night.
God bless for summer's sunshine
But now it's summer's end,
Sights of grace were so divine
Wait next year's come again.

Powell's That Be

What did you think of Conan the Barbarian Powell
When the powers that be had him on T.V.
Was it a proud to be a Afro American Black man
Or a he's sleeping with the enemy.

Everyday on the box talking about what was what
Scaremongering over Anti-American leanings,
Like the Lost Boys yet with his medal lion ribbons,
Seems caring that Powell,
But ultimately only for rich Americans living.

Armada

Sailed into my harbour
Shoot you out the water,
Once we were allies and
rallied together for temporary supplies.
Fought together never really
Comfortable with each other,
Had a pact but on separate tracks
To keep afloat was a cut throat business.

Had third parties to stop the arguing
Fated tho to end with bad feeling,
Now you're treading uncharted waters
Do my best to try to save ya.
Can we be amicable to each other?
I'll stretch my hand so reach for it,
For peace abound around this town
Can and will leave you uplifted.

One Blood

One blood, one blood, a whah dem a chant
To live in unity, love, peace and harmony
The end commodity. But I put dis to unnuh,
Destruction is where we're heading
Cussing and gunning for respect for the money,
To live like da whitey wid the fame and da
glory.
But it's not really possible with its illusion and
instability,
Dat whah dem a want, can we see it, no we
can't.
We're too busy being greedy den revert back
to our chant,
One blood when we feel like Momma Africa is
our life,
But den still divided a Caribbean wid a African
wife.
Dats a no go only for show, but with
togetherness
We would surely grow and rise surprisingly,
Then one blood would mean one blood, for us
all.

Such Is Love, For Two

Such is love we crumble for it,
Such is love head over heels for it,
Such is love it can control you,
Such is love it can annoy you.

Such is love we hurt by it,
Such is love always searching for it,
Truly find it are doves to its coo,
Such is love, such is love times two.

Such Is Love, For One

Such is love we succumb to it,
Such is love fall over leaves for it,
When we get love we take it for granted
Until it's gone then we pine for it again.

Hunger for love we lose weight over it,
Pile on the pounds to engross ourselves with it,
Dream always and hope it lasts forever,
Walk in hand for the greener side of it.

Land of Fear

Volley! Volley!
Saved by keepers
Too frightened of
The sight of reapers
They coming forth
To quench the thirst
Of Devil's lust
Who coverts first,
For souls do wail
From battered wars
And cries do hail
Some boxed to shore
Be homeward bound
But deaf to ears
To see no more
This land of fear.

Always Yours

Hi Julie,
Nice and sunny here
Wish you were here
To see this wonderful view,
Sure it would cheer you up
From your recent loss.
The sky is so crisp
The clouds so fluffed up,
Reminds me of that time
Me, you and your father
Smoked you know what
On a balcony in Alicante.
Funny that,
Smoked chimneys the three of us
Really clogged up our arteries,
Your dad gave up eventually
And within five weeks he was gone.
He would have loved it here
Watching the world edge by
With the glare in your eyes,
Miss you and see you soon.
Love,
Always yours.

C'est la Vie

I think of home, the fresh smell of air
My wife, my son (my petit pois.)
But here now in London
I drown my sorrows, for tomorrow,
I know not what comes,
If I go back to front to live
To fight another day.
Visualise home that I miss, my friends,
I know not where or if alive.
Best not think of tomorrow
Just live for today, c'est la vie.

Be Enhanced

Which side of the wire
Do I desire?
Is it the humdrum or the wondrous.

The humdrum,
Always negative energy
Never positive credited
Easily irritated
A victim in the making.

The wondrous,
Never nameless or infamous
Positive attitude and fearless
A stepper to the better
Enhances to succeed,

SO LIVE MY LIFE
NOT LIFE LEAVE ME.

Anything But

I'm anything but,
Everything I think of,
Everything I love,
I seem to mistrust.

I'm anything but,
Happened on purpose,
Must have
It was never luck.

I'm anything but,
Mind runs amok but
I keep it in check,
My mind that is,
It's anything but.

Mad Perceptions

Mad perceptions of mad professors
Making their promises to change the world,
Making mayhem of mass destructions
Till earth's collision to another world.
Those mad professors profess to differ
With other boffins them big headed girls,
Wish they could see what we all see
With good intentions we hurt ourselves.

The war to end all wars

It was the war to end all wars
Or so it was thought,
Nobody imagined that situation
Recurring from memories taught.

We're only now realising
The traumatic and harrowing
Grimace of war,
Shell shocked frightened sober
Shot for desertion
No matter what for.

While glamorised propaganda
Back home it would capture
The mood of the people
"See the world, to end all wars."

Overstan

Rastaman nah tek nah nonsense
From anyone widout question,
Dis you muss understand,
Dis I affi mention.

We love de chicken wing
De thigh dem, nah bony leg
Breast flesh we a want,
We chant fi Sharon,
We a want sexy Karen.

We conscious nah brok back mountain
Strictly woman we a deal wid,
Dis you muss understand
We rampant wid de gal dem
Do you overstan.

Who I Be

Still fighting my demons
One by one two by four
As many as they come,
Chewing them up and
Spitting them out no doubt.

Steady building columns,
No to hesitation
Till I get belief back,
Then forth to my horizon
Happy with who I be.

Them Changes

Love never changes but going thru changes,
Evaluating, readjusting, need to change
Turn the page new slate can't wait
Until later for things to alter.
Take charge and light brigade it
For you're the only one brave for you so
Find a way and ring those changes.

The Crowd

I can run wild against the crowd
Nobody knowing what's inside,
Communication, superficial smiles
Running nowhere running scared.
Wish they could hear my inner screams
Playing with my can of worms,
Intoxicating infected mind
Opening up against the crowd.

You Need Hands

Without our limbs to keep us in
We're cumbersome all legs and arms,
Without our arms to join one with
Our opposites with one less rib.
With one more fruit to clear our throat
Our differences are there to see,
Who mirror back with smiles to charm
Kiss face to face link arm in arm.

Rossen's Bench

Rossen's bench
Has been carved
Through the ages
Just as other Oaks
Had been chipped
Away at with time.
What's left is a
Timeless piece,
To stand alone
In Cambers Park
As the tree it was from
Had once stood.

The Buffalo Brings Death

The Buffalo brings death
See it in his eyes,
If he looks dead eye
Death comes more swiftly.

The Buffalo brings death
But to the native Indian
Vital to their existence
For the meat for the skin.

But must never doubt
He is always revered
And respected even
In his death.

So never lock horns
With the Buffalo
Because he can bring death
But also breeds life.

We Are

We are automation we are familiar
We are one voice under one cloud.

When it rains are moist together
And when dry are brittle of bones,
We smash we crash we rain down
Then back to cloud in our grey area.

We are thunder
We are lightning bolt.

True Colours

True colours.
Not that length today
Or any day I'm afraid,
Haven't read the small print
In black ink at the bottom.
She didn't either
Not that colour neither
But only true school colours
to be a true patriot.
Take perfect prefect here
Who always looks immaculate,
Never a hair out of place
Always fitting in no matter what.

Calling

When all is done and dusted
And clouds have gone astray,
Ships a cast and rusted
O will stop the day.

When sun goes into sunset
The moon comes out to play,
The night a dark and musty
The ground a laid to waste.

When light calls out so dimly
And hell calls in at haste
Tap knocking on our doorstep
The truth we'll have to face.

Crossed Words

Man Down.
The **wet rider** blew his **boa**
It was **easy** but he was **tested**,
He was a **brazen animal**.

Woman Across.
She wanted his chaser
To **taste** her **bread**
And **scan** her **hem rigid**.
He took off his **belt**,
And her **bra**,
He **winced** at what he saw.
She had him in her **claptrap**
For ages, then they held,
Complete they **paraded**
Never to be apart **again**.

Son-Shine

Life has not forsaken thee
Are always embers glowing,
My not know you are to me
Inspiration of adoring.
Have my utmost admiration
Standing strong for everyone,
Know your heart and all frustrations
As tears fall at light's dawn.

Thy sun will always shine
In thine eyes to his summit,
Worry not tho sweet divine
For everything will cometh.
The good things the bad things
They will always be entwined,
By ascending all life's junctures
Will descend into good times.

Sirens

Fatherless children
Unhappy together
Crying for daddy
From dusk to dawn.

Warring all over
Why is the question
Raining all over
With moon looking on.

Mist coming over
Battlegrounds venom
Red is the colour
As bang goes the drum.

Storm in a tea cup
Ruff in the trenches
Rotten and bloodless
As widows wail songs.

These Hands

These hands have wrestled humble
These hands will do good work
These hands are nothing but trouble
If hands can inherit their worth.

These hands have tested hot water
These hands can also be soiled
These hands they have the potential
To strangle the life from this world.

What's Done is Done

Think I care what you do to me?
It's all been done already
From intruding on my land
To taking my thoughts
So I do understand.

Think I care what you do to me?
Kill me, see if I care
Blind me, so I can't see
Think I can't see
What you've done to me.

Ravaging, raping,
Putting the sword in
Snarling at my ending.
But it's you who'll pay
For what was done to me.
Independently seething
Letting the whole world in
Liberally fleeing to be free
Of what was done to me.

Blaze a Trail

Blaze a trail in a black blazer,
Rather tho would wear
Top hat and tails like
Fred Astaire so debonair.
In class asked a calculation
I'd jump on the table top dancing
My answer drummed out in tap.
Instead of getting the cane
I'd use mine in waves and chains
Of musical veins,
To bring to the masses, the classes,
To teachers and headmasters,
To blaze my trail
In top hat and tails.

Tidal Shore

Pandemonium caused from the brawl
Creeping up on me as I sleep,
From nights before pub crawl
Water edged and dreary dream.
Skinny dipped with stain of blood
Laughing as foot soiled with mud,
Woken up drink sopped us out
Cold of heart wide of mouth.
Sprinkle salty faced it off
Remember sporadically night before,
Warm of scarf jerk of cough
Walking slowly skirts of shore.

Winter's End

Winter's end and up with the Larks
Wipe those eyes in waters blue.
Everything's stirring
Autumn's feed has done
Time to carry on
Roused from hibernation.
Feeling the first rays of sun on backs
What to be alive, what to be free again.

About my love

I could tell you all about my love
But words could not all justify
Could cling to love like words above
With heart a beating fast with joy.

I could write down all about my love
With pages creased with words abound
With hand I write fits like a glove
To her I answer her my all.

Best show you how I love my love
My heart is bigger than a star
My love flies over moon lit skies
On high to reach you where you are.

Stone Cold

Down the stony steps I go
Timid, slow and with caution,
Down, down, where cold doth blow
And damp met moss apportion.

Many a tale that would be told
Of spirit apparitions
Many a man had been so bold
For faint heart loves affection.

Highnesses and Blacknesses

Without a clue I'm Mr. Mustard
Some call me dirty old bastard.
But still I strive to stay alive
So give myself high fives,
Is that too old fashion talk
For the young who carry guns
Blasting holes in the tums
of a fellow brother man.
"BLOOD," you say,
When greeting fellow blacknesses
Yet still defeatist in ghetto faeces
When killing our black highnesses.
"One more dead,"
And a laugh from all the racists
That's their basis of hatred,
So should we stand for this?
No matter what the beef
Killing another should matter,
Should make your heart bleed
WORSE,
Most are our own black brothers.

Fancy Dan

Paranormal suicidal
Paranoid android,
Slave to its rhythm
Blind in real time.
Much to unravel unwind
On tides and mini ripples,
Revelational scepticism
Guzzled oceanic tipples.

Had me spoilt for choice I fancy
Must be the joker downtown
Real time punch drunk dandy
Round, head round, yes all around.

Globe in Our Hands

Gone in sixty seconds
In a blink of an eye
Rehearsal, upon rehearsal,
Upon rehearsal,
Till we got it right.
A British cup of tea
Then a big sigh,
Had the globe in our hands
If only for that day.

Give the dog a bone

I'm the be more dog
It's the dog in me,
From two years past
Back to the last century.

Sniffing here sniffing there
Led by masters everywhere,
Is it the dog's fault when he bolts
Viciously yappin' at others throats.

When you're trained in the brain
To go for the jugular vein,
Can you know another side
But cloudy rage.

It's the masters who control
And wears the crown,
But ultimately it's the dogs
Who always get put down

Face the Hun

Not up to speed John Parr
Died on par with millions,
And all sorts of minions
Broken hearts of Midlothians.

Your country needed you
And the Kitchener sink,
With eyes and pointed finger
Making faint hearts faint.

Brothers Grimm died together
Most face down in the mud,
All manner of men joined forces
Rallying round to fight the Hun.

Owen's Embankment

I'm banking on
The embankment home
Where breath exhaled
Shelled there to drone.
My sorrows bleed
With letters wrote
In muddled deep
With scrambled words.

Original

Mister follow fashion
Don't give a damn
Never an original
Always teethin' tings.

Making a quick buck
Not putting nothin' back
Following the trends
And out for himself.

But back gon bite you
When changes are needed
Stand alone feeling blue
Not knowing what to do.

Envisage

You may not believe what
I am about to reveal to you,
But I beg you bear with it.
For what you will find
Will stand you in good stead.

Imagine....

Written in the Skies

In the clouds I see
The shapes of all my enemies
All too many after me,
Then they break away
To plot and form another day
When I'm feeling grey.

Look again to the heavens
I see my salvation
That only I see,
Everybody else's venom
Waits in the background
To strike at me.

On the downside
Of a deep depression
The only way is up,
On the lee-side I have shelter
From another's umbrella
But ultimately,
I face the skies alone.

Twisted

Glide around like headless chickens
In listed buildings to space you out,
Soar above the pivotal kisses
Of distant visits from wolves who pout.

Kiss it like a twisted biscuit
To lift the spirits and better the highs,
Guard from wicked tired bitches
In soft yellow britches who wrong not right.

Train Hopping

Going insane
Waiting for a train,
I am in pain
Running for a train.

Hustles and bustles
Cramming our muscles
Into black tunnels
In packs of clear wax.

Reaching our destinations
As honey bees networking
To work for our labour
Till the end of our days.

In the Mood

Blue mood
I feel in a blue mood,
The wrong side of
I got out of today.
That slow mood
Blue moon
In my dark room
Black dogs at it again.

Snap out!
I here them shout
Voices here
Are what's in here,
Repeat again,
What are you saying?
It rains here, reigns
Before it pours.

Undoubted

Madness is a sadness of paranoia that'll destroy ya,
Sanity is the manageability of worries that won't
control thee,
Weakness is a stress you give into in your abyss
While strength is the wealth in a trench you dig
deep into.

Trust is the must you have at your epicentral crust
While lies are a tirade of flies that you must keep
swatting,
For me life's a trial whatever way I'm living
But faith is in abundance, of that I am undoubting.

Sometimes a Pessimist

Sometimes a pessimist.
Minds drained, can I make it better?
Here we go again, wrote it down in this letter.
Sniff this Charlie, am I barking?
Browned off now, now realising.
Take the bait each and everytime
Can't relent from falling down,
Strong will in some things here still
But am I living? Shaky from past dealings
Are what make me depressed,
Revelations got me bleeding
Are what make me a pessimist.

Who We Be

Here we go again back in my own pig-pen
Nervously twitching always alert watching,
Hoping wistfully that i'm wrong totally
About paranoid feelings that are deep rooted.

Seeped in burning oil biting me vigorously
Manhandling me ravaging my territory
Savaging my personality, but still I'm just me
So not who I want to be.

Last Orders Please

Toiling hard for this day
Ringing bell tune in time,
Liquid quenching the thirst
At the end of the line.
They ogling over the lasses
As the clock beckons on
Wiping lips from glasses
As the night spirits on.
Piano man plays a swan song
Now abrupt in my speech,
For the umpteenth time of asking
Last orders if you please.

I'm Not Making Any Sense?

I'm not making any sense,
Write down to make sense,
I'm not pleading innocence
I just want to make sense.
See me rushing past your door
Rushing round forever lost
STOP! to think don't think no more
This is what my life has cost.
Hope there's someone watching me
Over me, over me watching,
On high someone over me.
Now free at last free at last,
Free to scan what's gone before
Free to move ahead of myself
Free to judge, and judged I be.

Disruptive Spirits

He's a disruptive old spirit
Drink all day then vomit,
On it a jolly old soul
Gulp down a bottomless pit.
Not in his spirits he's
A moody old sod,
A light to a match,
Like a pig to a trough.
The truth all bears out
When he's there swigging
A much nicer person than
That disruptive old spirit.

It's All Here.

Is white pure?
White and black equal
A very grey area,
Very grey area
In jungles green
Lead to mass confusion,
Mass confusion leaves you
Sorry and blue, bruised,
Blackened and tainted.
Can't you see?
It's all here laid out
In black and white.

Beautiful Dream

The beautiful dream for me
Happened years ago,
The optimist lives only
A back of the bus away.
Was kept in my eye-line tho
Back in my pram tantalizing,
Born in the sixties
And I still hold that dream today.

Away From The Flock

The lord is my shepherd
I've been away from the flock,
He's also made me lay down
Sometimes alone in Hyde Park.

Been led to the Thames Water
Considering ending my soul,
Guided back to the flock now
After years away for flocks sake.

Think of death but don't fear it tho
And I've been made strong,
For the black sheep they comfort me
From been a outsider for so long.

Voices were my enemy
And led to paranoia,
"Douse ya head and light it,"
They said, "It'll destroy ya."

But I'm still here waiting
Waiting for my guiding light
Must be someone watching
Over this black sheep by night.

All that we the black sheep want
Is just to be understood,
So be believers and set us free
Free from the the chains that bind us.

Blank Space

I look at a blank page
And I see infinite possibilities,
So many ideas
I could write down.
So much to uplift
Or to dis, to ravage
A nation, to debate,
To envelope to hand down.

I look at a blank page
Not premeditated as this ain't
But my thoughts written down
As they come what may
What may not, and I realize.
It's controlled like a mobile
A blank screen but
Push the button of control
And it drags you in
Sucks your brain engrosses,
Just like a blank page waits,
Waits to be written.

No Jaywalking

No jaywalking
No hawking
Spam making
SILIENCE! I'm talking
Clash of words
Belly rumbling
Rush of blood
At apple crumbling
Stomach swelling
Birth a calling pitter patter
Heart is churning,
So fast running
Trip now I'm falling
Should have known
No jaywalking.

Soap Suds

"How could you do this
To me and with her,
After all we've been through?"

"Who's he?"

"Shut up! you hussy,
I'm band, Husband.
Can I join in?"

Round Here

Desolate round here where
Faces are blurred out
Anonymous to each other.
No-one smiles cos, if you
Do smile you're not normal
As no-one smiles anymore
In this drab and dreary
Yet spirited city.
I travel with cold and callous
Seats of people, fanatically
Clutching their phones as
Thou clutching a Bible
Or something else sacred.
Through the window
There's a man by a cul-de-sac
Knowing, if he dare walk down there
He has no hope.
Seated front and centre riding shotgun
Is Dead-End Johnny,
Going no-where fast but still upbeat
Humming a line to pass the time
Oblivious of all that surrounds him.
While Sister Sarah rants
Firmly but quietly

Rocking back and forth
Praying for her salvation.
But I see things differently as in
I dare to look beyond the cul-de-sac
And I see hope.
Johnny Cash sways going somewhere
Humming a bar of his rhymes
To all that surrounds him,
And Sister Sarah, she ain't so peculiar,
Praying for each and every
Travelling somebodies seated
Feeling Johnny's tune. So really
We only see what we want to see
Round here, round here, round here.

Double Take

Bodkin Beedlebum
Needling the eye of
Ire from my dire straits
Sultan of the human race.
Stripping up a knife blade
Swordfish double edged
Vodka altered vomit states
Double outing double take.

Fitting In

Always wanted to fit in,
But the older I got
The more I was fine
With the skin I'm in.
Back in my teens
I remember being so
Accommodating even
Held on to the has beens.
So called friend strung me along
For o so long, for the crack,
For the fun of it.
Still a Plain Jane now
But now I have incite,
Matters not my hang-ups
As any shape I want to be in
I for myself fit in.

Georgia

Georgia on my mind
Seventh of its kind
Related to my speech
Brought up on its knees.
Taught me bout life's cycles
Repairing trodden tyres
Right from wrong to balance
Steering forward motions.
So always on my mind
Seventh of its kind
Relative to my speech
Brought up on its knees.

Calm After the Storm

I lay there panting
Trussed up like a chicken
Pondering my ending
And how it had got to this.
Anger takes me over
As the drugs take effect,
Bringing a calm after
The storm. Soon be asleep
And wince in my dreams,
Then awake and ache
Seeing my captors
Wafting pills before my eyes.

Changling

Time is a changing and
I'm changing with time,
No time for wasting
Am living to dream.

Don't need no overhauling
I'm managing my mental health
But what I really need
Is to **BE**lieve in **MYSELF**.

Wishful Thinking

I wish I were a
Man for all seasons
And had reasons
For crying, and not be
Cold to the scorch.
I wish I could love
Madly, intravenously
All pumping wanting
To marry you off.

Hanging from rafters
From mornings after
Waiting for your letter
From pillar to post.
Just yearning
Pulling out hair strings
Biting the bullet
In a shot if you want.

Johnboy and Belle

Johnboy Walton and
Mary Baby Belle
Fell in love
One summers spell.
Johnboy loved being away
With the fairies especially
With the Belle named Mary.
Mary was his
One and only,
Johnboy loved her
So contrary.

So up the hill
One day they went
She had a bump
For 9 months hence,
But a happy ending
Never befell
Johnboy Walton and
Mary Baby Belle.

Just for You

When I feel good about myself
It's because of you,
When I dress to impress
It's for your eyes only.
So when you're feeling down
And a frown is coming on,
Think of these few things
And a smile I'm sure will ensue.

Cut to the Chase

Spiralling down down
Drowning out now
The life that's left.
Always drowning really
Zombie walking through life
Jive talking, mumbling,
Bumbling through it all.
What's the point?
In all that in-between
From birth to death
When it all ends
In the same way.
Shame we can't just
Cut to the chase

Next Low-down

How could he?
Brotherly love and all,
Stabbed me in the back
Made me take a pause
And check myself.
Was it my fault?
Was I a sitting duck?
Was I a money bank?
A piggy in the middle
With him on one side
Lucy on the sky side
With diamond out eyes
When he was high.
"Experience it myself,"
I cried, see what it's like,
But no, leave well alone
For the Hyenas, Lions, Tigers,
Vultures crooking around
Waiting for the next low-down.

Give me grace

Reverence, give me reverence
Penance the healing of.
Moodiest, moodiest of fellows
Capitulation I'm fleeing from.

Give me grace,
Grace to face their onslaught
And lessons learnt
From biting their bark.

Brain capsiznig
Paranoid to trot,
From incessant notions
And potions they concoct.

So give me grace
And I will face anything,
From the tallest of stories
To the gravest of lies.

Lightning Source UK Ltd.
Milton Keynes UK
UKOW04f0406281115

263683UK00001B/3/P